Trinny Woodall: The Style Icon

Trinny Woodall is a British fashion advisor, television presenter, and entrepreneur. She is best known for her work in the fashion and beauty industry. Trinny Woodall gained fame as one half of the fashion and makeover duo "Trinny and Susannah" (the other half being Susannah Constantine). Together, they hosted a number of popular television shows, including "What Not to Wear" and "Trinny & Susannah Undress." These shows offered fashion and style advice to people looking to improve their personal image.

Trinny Woodall has also written books on fashion and style, including "What Not to Wear" and "The Body Shape Bible." She has been a fashion columnist and has contributed to various magazines and newspapers. In addition to her work in the fashion world, she has also ventured into the beauty industry and launched her own makeup and skincare line.

Trinny Woodall was born on February 8, 1964, in London, England. Before her career as a fashion advisor and television presenter, she worked in various roles in the fashion and media industries. Trinny met her longtime collaborator, Susannah Constantine, in the late 1990s, and they went on to create a successful partnership that focused on helping individuals with their personal style and fashion choices.

"Trinny & Susannah" gained widespread recognition and became known for their candid and often blunt approach to style makeovers. They provided advice on clothing choices, makeup, and overall personal image. The duo's television shows, including "What Not to Wear," were well-received and had international versions in several countries.

In addition to her television work and fashion advice, Trinny Woodall has written books on fashion, body image, and personal style, sharing her expertise with a broader audience. Her books and TV shows encouraged people to embrace their own unique styles and feel more confident in their appearance.

Trinny's ventures expanded to include her own cosmetics and skincare line called "Trinny London," which she launched in 2017. The brand is known for its makeup products and innovative approach to helping customers find the right makeup shades and products for their skin tone and type.

Trinny Woodall's career and influence in the fashion and beauty industry have made her a recognized figure in the UK and beyond. Her work has contributed to the ongoing conversation about personal style and body positivity. Please note that for the most up-to-date information about her career and activities, you may want to refer to more recent sources or her official website.

In addition to her work on television and in the fashion and beauty industry, Trinny Woodall has maintained a strong presence on social media and various online platforms. She has a substantial following on platforms like Instagram and YouTube, where she shares style tips, beauty tutorials, and product recommendations. Through her online presence, she continues to engage with her audience and offer valuable advice on fashion, makeup, and self-confidence.

Trinny Woodall is known for her no-nonsense, body-positive approach to fashion and beauty. She encourages people to embrace their individuality and feel confident in their own skin. Her work has been instrumental in promoting self-esteem and self-expression in the world of fashion.

Furthermore, Trinny Woodall's career has evolved over the years, and she has adapted to changing trends and technologies in the fashion and beauty industries. Her transition into the online and e-commerce space with the launch of "Trinny London" demonstrates her ability to stay relevant and innovative in the business world.

Trinny Woodall's impact on fashion and style is not only reflected in her television shows and books but also in her ongoing efforts to empower individuals to feel better about themselves through the way they present themselves to the world.

Early Life and Nickname

Trinny Woodall, born Sarah-Jane Duncanson Woodall on February 8, 1964, in Marylebone, London, is a British beauty entrepreneur, businesswoman, fashion expert, television presenter, and author. Her journey into the world of fashion and beauty began with a nickname. At the tender age of five, she was playfully dubbed "Trinny" by family friend Frank Launder, the director of the St Trinian films. This charming moniker stuck, and little did anyone know it would become synonymous with fashion and style. The nickname arose after Trinny was sent home from school for an innocent misadventure - cutting off another little girl's plait.

Rising to Fame with Susannah Constantine

Trinny's path to stardom was defined by her partnership with Susannah Constantine. In 1996, the dynamic duo collaborated on "Ready to Wear," a weekly style guide for The Daily Telegraph, which they successfully ran for seven years. Their guide focused on affordable high-street fashion, with the two women often modeling the clothing themselves to demonstrate styles that complemented different body shapes. Trinny took on the role of stylist and made key business decisions for the partnership.

Their collaboration extended to television, where they became household names as co-hosts and fashion advisors for the BBC series "What Not to Wear." Their combination of fashion knowledge and candid advice made the show a hit. In 2002, they received a prestigious Royal Television Society Award for Best Factual Presenter for their work on "What Not to Wear." The show itself received nominations for the Features Award at the BAFTA Awards in 2002 and 2003.

Their popularity transcended borders as they often shared their makeover and fashion expertise on "The Oprah Winfrey Show," especially on BBC America.

After their successful run on the BBC, the dynamic duo transferred to ITV, where they began their new show, "Trinny & Susannah Undress..." in 2006. Throughout their careers, they also made regular appearances on shows like "This Morning," "The Today Show," and "The Marilyn Denis Show."

The Author Duo

Trinny Woodall and Susannah Constantine have co-authored numerous fashion advice books, with a combined worldwide sales figure of over 3 million copies. Their books have been translated and sold in various countries, earning them the top spots on The Sunday Times best-seller list and The New York Times best-seller list.

Trinny London: The Beauty Brand

In 2017, Trinny Woodall ventured into the world of beauty entrepreneurship by founding Trinny London, a direct-to-consumer beauty brand. The brand's mission is to help people "rethink their routine" with personalized makeup and skincare products. In a short span of five years, Trinny London grew to become one of the fastest-growing beauty businesses in Europe, employing over 190 people

Awards and Accolades

Throughout her career, Trinny Woodall has received numerous awards and recognitions for her contributions to the fashion and beauty industry. These include accolades such as Woman & Home Beauty Awards, Positive Luxury Awards, Natwest Every Woman Awards, CEW Achiever Awards, and many more.

Personal Life

Trinny Woodall's personal life has seen its share of highs and lows. She was married to entrepreneur and former drummer Jonathan Elichaoff in 1999, with whom she had a daughter around 2003. Unfortunately, their marriage ended in divorce in 2009 after two years of separation. The divorce settlement took an unexpected turn, resulting in a complex and novel legal case in 2016. Elichaoff's bankruptcy before the divorce's finalization led to legal attempts to void the settlement, but the claim was ultimately rejected by the High Court.

Trinny Woodall's journey from a schoolgirl with a mischievous nickname to a prominent figure in the world of fashion, beauty, and television demonstrates her resilience, creativity, and impact on the industry. Her passion for empowering individuals to embrace their style and redefine their beauty routines has left an enduring mark on the fashion world.

Continued Legacy and Impact

Trinny Woodall's remarkable journey from an early misadventure at school to the heights of fashion and beauty entrepreneurship is a testament to her enduring passion and resilience. Her impact on the fashion and beauty industry is immeasurable, with millions of individuals inspired to embrace their unique style and redefine their beauty routines.

Her role as a fashion advisor and TV presenter not only helped transform the wardrobes of countless people but also bolstered the idea that style and self-confidence go hand in hand. Trinny and Susannah's candid, straight-talking approach resonated with viewers, offering a refreshing departure from the often pretentious world of high fashion.

Trinny's venture into the beauty industry with Trinny London brought a new level of personalization to makeup and skincare. By encouraging people to rethink their beauty routines and providing them with tailor-made products, she has empowered individuals to feel confident and comfortable in their own skin. Trinny London's rapid growth and numerous awards underline the success of her unique approach to beauty.

Despite personal challenges, including a high-profile divorce and legal proceedings, Trinny Woodall has demonstrated resilience and determination. Her legal battle showcased her unwavering commitment to principles and values, garnering respect from both supporters and observers.

With her continued involvement in television, fashion, and beauty, Trinny Woodall remains an influential figure who inspires individuals to embrace their authenticity, redefine their style, and celebrate their inner and outer beauty.

As she continues to evolve her career and brand, there is no doubt that Trinny Woodall will leave a lasting legacy in the worlds of fashion and beauty, inspiring generations to come to explore their unique styles and redefine their beauty routines.

Embracing the Future

Trinny Woodall's journey has been marked by innovation, transformation, and the unwavering pursuit of her passions. While her career has already left a significant mark on the fashion and beauty industries, she shows no sign of slowing down. With a thriving beauty brand, Trinny London, and her continued presence in the media, she is poised to embrace the future with enthusiasm and creativity.

Trinny London's rapid ascent in the beauty business reflects not only her entrepreneurial acumen but also her dedication to enhancing the lives of people through personalized makeup and skincare. This direct-to-consumer approach has disrupted the beauty industry, providing a refreshing alternative to one-size-fits-all products. Trinny's commitment to helping individuals "rethink their routine" remains at the heart of her brand's success.

In the ever-evolving world of fashion and beauty, Trinny Woodall's influence extends far beyond her television appearances and best-selling books. Her unique perspective and approach to style and self-expression have helped shape the way people perceive themselves and their personal image. Her ability to cut through the noise and offer honest, practical advice has resonated with millions, making her a true icon in the indus

Personal challenges have only served to reinforce Trinny's determination and integrity. Her legal battle over a divorce settlement showcased her unwavering commitment to principles and fairness. While personal trials can be trying, they have not deterred her from pursuing her passions and leaving an indelible mark on the world.

As Trinny Woodall moves forward, it is clear that her impact will only continue to grow. Her ability to inspire individuals to embrace their authentic selves, redefine their style, and celebrate their inner and outer beauty is a legacy that transcends time and trends. In an industry often dominated by the superficial, she remains a beacon of authenticity and empowerment.

The future holds great promise for Trinny Woodall, and her story is far from finished. As she continues to innovate, empower, and inspire, she will undoubtedly play a pivotal role in shaping the fashion and beauty landscape for generations to come.

A Vision for the Future

Trinny Woodall's journey from a schoolgirl with a quirky nickname to a renowned figure in the fashion and beauty industry is a testament to her unwavering commitment to her craft. She has already left an indelible mark, but the future holds even more potential for this multifaceted entrepreneur, author, and television personality.

In a world where the beauty and fashion industries are constantly evolving, Trinny continues to be at the forefront of innovation. Her beauty brand, Trinny London, represents a bold departure from conventional makeup and skincare, advocating for individuality and self-expression. As consumers increasingly seek personalized experiences, Trinny's brand is well-positioned to meet these demands and revolutionize the beauty market further.

Trinny's legacy extends beyond her business ventures. Her fearless and candid approach to fashion advice has inspired a generation to embrace their unique style, regardless of their age, body shape, or budget. She has dismantled the barriers that often separate individuals from their authentic selves and has shown that fashion is a tool for empowerment, not exclusion.

While her personal challenges have been well-documented, they have only fueled her determination. Trinny Woodall remains an exemplar of resilience and integrity, always staying true to her principles. This steadfast commitment to what she believes in has earned her respect and admiration, making her not just a style icon but a role model for many.

As she looks ahead to the future, one can only speculate about what Trinny Woodall will achieve next. Her story is far from over, and her influence continues to grow. In an industry often defined by fleeting trends and superficiality, she stands as a symbol of authenticity and empowerment.

In the ever-evolving world of fashion and beauty, Trinny Woodall is not just a trendsetter; she is a trailblazer. Her story is a testament to the power of self-belief, personal style, and the enduring impact one individual can have on an entire industry and the lives of countless people. As she continues to innovate, empower, and inspire, Trinny Woodall's future is as bright and bold as the unique beauty she has encouraged in others.

A Legacy of Empowerment

Trinny Woodall's life and career have been characterized by a steadfast commitment to empowering others. From her early days as a makeover maven to her pioneering role in the beauty industry, she has consistently championed individuality, authenticity, and self-expression. As the story of her life unfolds, we can only anticipate that her legacy will grow in depth and breadth.

In an era where societal pressures to conform to narrow beauty standards are ever-present, Trinny has been a beacon of authenticity. Her career is a testament to the idea that fashion and beauty are not about conforming, but rather about celebrating our uniqueness. Her work has encouraged people to embrace their flaws, quirks, and individuality, recognizing that these qualities are what truly make them beautiful.

The success of Trinny London, her direct-to-consumer beauty brand, showcases her visionary approach to personalization. As consumers increasingly seek products tailored to their unique needs and preferences, Trinny has been ahead of the curve, offering an alternative to the one-size-fits-all beauty industry. Her brand has not only disrupted the market but also challenged established norms.

While Trinny's career achievements are significant, her personal journey through challenges and triumphs has touched the hearts of many. Her resilience in the face of adversity, including her high-profile divorce and ensuing legal battles, serves as a reminder that even in our darkest hours, we can find the strength to persevere.

Looking ahead, it is clear that Trinny Woodall's influence will continue to evolve and expand. Her dedication to empowering individuals to celebrate their true selves, to embrace their unique style, and to redefine their beauty routines is a legacy that transcends trends and generations.

In an industry often dominated by superficiality, Trinny Woodall remains a powerful voice for authenticity and self-empowerment. As she continues to pave the way for future generations, her story serves as an enduring reminder that true beauty is about embracing who we are, and this journey is something that never goes out of style.

Charting New Horizons

Trinny Woodall's journey is far from reaching its conclusion; it is an ongoing narrative of inspiration, innovation, and empowerment. As she looks towards the future, there are exciting horizons waiting to be explored and milestones yet to be achieved.

With Trinny London at the forefront of the beauty industry's transformation, there is no doubt that Trinny's pioneering spirit will continue to drive innovation. The brand's personalized approach to makeup and skincare will likely set the standard for how beauty products are designed, marketed, and experienced. As the demand for individualized beauty solutions grows, Trinny Woodall's brand is poised to remain at the forefront of this exciting shift.

Beyond her role as a businesswoman, Trinny's legacy as a fashion and style icon continues to evolve. Her fearless and candid approach to fashion advice, whether through her books or television appearances, continues to break down barriers and encourage self-expression. The message she spreads—that fashion is a tool for self-empowerment—is more relevant than ever in a world that increasingly values authenticity and diversity.

Her journey, marked by personal challenges and triumphs, further underscores the depth of her character and resilience. These experiences have made her not just a style icon but a symbol of strength and integrity. Trinny's determination to stand by her principles and the values she holds dear is a testament to her unwavering commitment to her beliefs.

As we anticipate what the future holds for Trinny Woodall, one thing is certain: her impact on the worlds of fashion, beauty, and self-empowerment will only continue to grow. Her story is an ever-unfolding narrative of inspiration, innovation, and resilience. In an industry often defined by fleeting trends and superficiality, Trinny Woodall stands as a beacon of authenticity and empowerment.

Leaving a Lasting Impression

Trinny Woodall's life story reads like a captivating novel filled with twists and turns, triumphs, and challenges. Yet, it's not the conclusion but the ongoing chapters of her journey that keep us all enthralled. As the pages of her life continue to be written, we can't help but wonder what she will accomplish next.

In a beauty and fashion landscape that is constantly evolving, Trinny's innovative spirit and vision are likely to chart new territory. Trinny London, her groundbreaking beauty brand, has demonstrated her ability to anticipate and fulfill the changing needs of consumers. With a dedication to personalization and self-expression at its core, it has disrupted the beauty industry. We can only expect it to evolve further, setting new standards for beauty products and experiences.

As an icon in the fashion world, Trinny's influence extends far beyond her television appearances and best-selling books. Her philosophy that fashion is a means of self-empowerment, a way to express one's authentic self, has resonated deeply with people of all backgrounds. She has shattered stereotypes and shown that beauty knows no age, size, or shape.

Throughout her life, Trinny has encountered challenges and triumphs, each chapter contributing to her remarkable story. Her unwavering determination and commitment to her principles, demonstrated in her legal battles, have solidified her reputation as a role model for integrity and resilience.

As we eagerly await the next pages of Trinny Woodall's story, one thing remains certain: her impact on the fashion and beauty worlds will continue to expand. Her unique ability to inspire individuals to embrace their true selves, express their personal style, and celebrate their inner and outer beauty is an enduring legacy that transcends time and trends.

In an industry often dominated by superficiality, Trinny Woodall remains a source of authenticity and empowerment. Her ongoing narrative serves as a reminder that true beauty is about embracing our unique selves, a journey that remains forever timeless and deeply resonant.

Inspiring Generations to Come

Trinny Woodall's story is far from reaching its final chapter; it's an ever-evolving narrative of inspiration and empowerment. As she peers into the future, the potential for her influence and impact knows no bounds.

Trinny's pioneering role in the beauty industry, with Trinny London at its forefront, is a testament to her ability to revolutionize the way we think about makeup and skincare. The personalized approach she champions has already disrupted the beauty landscape, and it's clear that this concept will continue to redefine the industry, setting new standards and expectations for beauty products tailored to individual needs and preferences.

Her legacy as a fashion and style icon is unwavering, and it's an ongoing journey. Through her candid and fearless approach, she continually breaks down barriers and promotes the idea that fashion is a means of self-empowerment, an avenue to express one's true self. Her message is particularly relevant in a world that increasingly celebrates authenticity and diversity.

Beyond her professional accomplishments, Trinny's personal trials have only added depth to her character and resilience. Her unwavering commitment to her principles and values is a testament to her strength and integrity. In the face of adversity, she has remained a symbol of determination and courage.

As we look forward to what lies ahead for Trinny Woodall, one thing is certain: her influence on the realms of fashion, beauty, and self-empowerment will continue to expand. Her life story is a compelling narrative of resilience, innovation, and inspiration. In an industry often characterized by fleeting trends and superficiality, Trinny Woodall shines as a beacon of authenticity and empowerment.

Her legacy, both in her business ventures and as a fashion and style icon, is an ongoing source of inspiration. Trinny Woodall's journey reminds us that true beauty is not about conforming to others' standards but celebrating our unique selves and embracing the journey of self-discovery. Her story is one that transcends time and trends, inspiring generations to come to embrace their authenticity and redefine their own path to beauty and self-expression.

Printed in Great Britain
by Amazon

35859778R00018